'Let's try the song once more, your Majesty,' said Billy the Butler.

'Right,' said Queen Norah. She sang,

'We're going to win the cup. We're going to win the cup. Ooh ah the addio, we're going to win the cup.

How was that?'

'Much better, your Majesty,' sighed Billy. 'But do try to…'

'Try to what?' snapped Queen Norah.

'Well,' said Billy. 'It would help if you sounded a little happier.'

'It's this song,' said Queen Norah. 'It's got such silly words. But our football team is in the cup final and I really must learn it.'

King Harry walked in.

'Do you think we will win, dear?'

'Of course we will,' said Queen
Norah.

'Yes dear,' said King Harry. 'But the
Carrot Castle team are such cheats,
especially King Charles, the manager.'

At that moment, Captain Jones marched in. 'I've just had a message from King Charles at Carrot Castle. He is very keen to know what colour shirts our team will be wearing.'

'Green, I think,' said King Harry. 'And his lot can play in red. Has anyone seen Princess Jane? I am going to run a training session for her after breakfast.'

Captain Jones giggled.

'And what's so funny?' asked the
King. 'In my younger days I was known
as the Wizard of the Dribble.'

'That,' said Queen Norah, 'was
because you couldn't eat rice pudding
without putting most of it down your
shirt.'

There was a crash of broken glass
from the hall.

'Sorry,' called Princess Jane. She came in carrying a football. 'I missed my kick.'

'Ah, Jane,' said Queen Norah. 'I was watching you in training yesterday. You didn't play well at all. Don't forget you are the team captain. So I have told one of the best trainers in the country to give you some help.'

King Harry blushed. 'I'm not quite that good.'

'Not you, you twit,' said Queen
Norah. 'Mr Goal.'

'Missed a goal?' said King Harry.
'Don't you mean "scored a goal"?'

'What are you talking about?' cried
Queen Norah. 'That's his name.
Mr Jason Goal. He's coming here this
morning. I must dash. I have to try on
my new football fan's outfit.'

The Queen rushed off.

2

The dining room fell silent.

'What's the matter, dear?' said King Harry.

Princess Jane let out a great long sigh.

'Mum's right. I'm not playing very well. I'm supposed to score goals. At the moment I couldn't score against a mouse.'

'On your head, Jane,' called King Harry and he threw the ball at the Princess. She jumped at the ball. The ball bounced off her shoulder into the marmalade.

'See what I mean?' she said sadly.

'Never mind,' said King Harry. 'By the time you've put your kit on, Mr Goal will be here. You'll soon be scoring dozens of goals. But now it's time for us to get to work.'

King Harry, Captain Smith and Captain Jones loved doing housework. Queen Norah thought that housework was a job for cleaners, not captains and kings. So once a week the three men disguised themselves as the Masked Cleaning Ladies of Om.

King Harry and his two captains raced out of the dining room. Minutes later, dusters in hands, and dressed as the famous cleaning ladies, they were at work tidying the castle.

King Harry and Captain Jones were polishing the cannons when they saw a man walking towards the castle.

'That must be Mr Goal,' said Captain Jones.

Just as Mr Goal reached the drawbridge another man jumped out of the bushes. He began talking with Mr Goal.

'Wait a minute,' said King Harry. 'It's King Charles of Carrot Castle.'

King Charles spoke to Mr Goal
and then walked away.

'What did he want?' asked Captain
Jones.

'There's something funny going on.
We'd better keep an eye on him,' said
King Harry.

King Harry and the two captains
cleaned around the castle for the rest of
the morning. But they made sure that
one of them was always watching
Princess Jane and Mr Goal.

The three cleaners stopped for a cup of tea in the kitchen.

'Well,' said King Harry. 'There doesn't seem to be anything funny going on.'

'I saw the Princess put the ball in the net dozens of times,' said Captain Jones.

'She was heading the ball perfectly when I went by,' said Captain Smith.

'There's nothing to worry about,' said King Harry. 'Now perhaps we can tackle the grime round the cooker.'

Princess Jane stuck her head round the door.

'How are things going, dear?' asked King Harry.

'Brilliantly,' said Princess Jane. 'I've never played better. I've just popped in to say that we're having one last training session. We will be in the library. Mr Goal says that he does not want anyone to come in.'

She was gone in a flash.

'That sounds a bit odd to me,'
said Captain Jones.

'Very odd,' agreed Captain
Smith.

'I think that it's time to polish
the brass,' said King Harry.

'The brass next to the library?'
said Captains Smith and Jones.

'Of course,' said King Harry.

'Well,' whispered King Harry, 'what can you see?'

Captain Jones was peering through the keyhole.

'They are sitting facing each other,' he said.

'Yes. Yes,' said King Harry.

'Now Mr Goal is swinging a watch on a chain, backwards and forwards,' said Captain Jones.

'He's telling the Princess about last-minute goals,' said Captain Smith.

'No he's not,' gasped Captain Jones. 'He is hypnotizing Princess Jane.'

'I wonder why?' said King Harry.

'To help her remember tactics,' said Captain Smith.

'I still don't like it,' said King Harry.

Princess Jane danced into the kitchen.

'He's gone.'

'How do you feel?' asked King Harry.

'Brilliant,' said Princess Jane. 'I feel ready to score loads of goals.'

'Jolly good,' said Captain Smith.

'I must go and work on my penalty kicks,' said Princess Jane. 'By the way, Captain Smith, I love your new overall.'

'Thank you, Princess.'

'Green really suits you,' laughed the Princess as she ran off to the garden.

The three cleaners looked at each other.

'Green!' they said together.

'But my overall's red,' said Captain Smith.

'It's that Mr Goal,' roared Captain
Jones. 'He's hypnotized her to think
that red is green.'

'Why does he want her to think
that?' asked King Harry.

'Because,' gasped Captain Jones,
'Carrot Castle are playing in red. If the
Princess thinks that red is green she will
pass to the Carrot Castle team instead
of ours.'

'So that's why King Charles was talking to Mr Goal,' said King Harry.

'Can't we snap her out of it?' asked Captain Smith. 'Can't we throw a bucket of water over her?'

'No,' said King Harry. 'That could be dangerous. I have a better idea. Follow me to Carrot Castle.'

The Masked Cleaning Ladies
stopped outside the kitchen of Carrot
Castle. Mrs Jumpkins was pegging out
the Carrot Castle red football shirts.
The cleaning ladies got off their
horses. They pretended to look at
the shirts.

'Oh dear,' said King Harry.

'Oh dear, oh dear,' added Captain
Jones and Captain Smith.

'What's the matter?' asked Mrs Jumpkins.

'When are you going to wash these shirts?' asked Captain Smith.

'What do you mean?' snapped Mrs Jumpkins. 'I'm just putting them out to dry.'

'You call this clean?' said Captain Jones.

'Yes I do,' said Mrs Jumpkins.

'It's the dungeon for you then,' said
King Harry.

'Dungeon?' said Mrs Jumpkins.
'What's the dungeon got to do with me?'

'That's where the last washerwoman
ended up,' said Captain Smith. 'And she
handed in shirts cleaner than this.'

'Oh my,' moaned Mrs Jumpkins.
'I haven't got the time to do them
again. The team are playing in the cup
final this afternoon.'

'Leave it to us,' said King Harry. 'We can wash, dry and iron these shirts in half an hour.'

Half an hour later the King handed a parcel to Mrs Jumpkins.

'There you are. All done. Now whatever you do, don't take the kit out of the bag until the team are ready to play. Then the shirts will look perfect.'

The two royal families took their places side by side in the royal box. Queen Norah looked amazing in her new football fan's outfit. She even had a hat in the shape of a football pitch.

The crowd cheered as the two teams ran out onto the pitch.

Princess Jane's team was in red and Carrot Castle was in green.

'Wait a minute,' gasped King Charles. 'The teams have got the wrong shirts. Carrot Castle are supposed to be in red.'

'Surely,' said King Harry, 'it doesn't matter what colours they play in? They must be different colours, that's all.'

King Charles put his head in his hands and groaned.

'Six nil. Six nil. Six nil,' chanted Queen Norah. 'Oh well done!'

'We are so proud of you, Jane,' laughed King Harry. 'Scoring all six goals.'

'It's all thanks to Mr Goal, my trainer,' said Jane. 'I must show him the cup.'

'Not today,' said Queen Norah. 'It is far too dirty. Nobody can see the cup until those cleaning ladies have given it a proper polish.'

'Yes dear,' said King Harry. 'I'll – I mean – they'll see to it next time they come.'

About the author

I was born in London in 1950
and now live by the seaside,
in Ramsgate. In the evening
I like to write stories and
poems. I do this very quietly.
Then I go downstairs and
play jazz records very loudly.
My family think that I do
two very daft things. One is

going up the garden every night looking for
frogs, newts and hedgehogs. The other is
supporting Gillingham Football Club.